Bipolar Disorder

Understanding and managing bipolar disorder, bipolar disorder remedies, treatments, and much more!

Table of Contents

Chapter 1 - Understanding Bipolar Disorder 1

Chapter 2 - Detecting the Signs and Symptoms of Bipolar Disorder 4

Chapter 3 - Bipolar Disorder Treatment: Pharmacological Therapy 9

Chapter 4 - Non-Pharmacological Management of Bipolar Disorder 13

Chapter 5 - Self-Help Strategies For Bipolar Disorder 19

Chapter 6 - Living with Bipolar Disorder 23

Conclusion 26

Introduction

I want to thank you and congratulate you for downloading the book, *"Bipolar Disorder"*.

This book contains helpful information about bipolar disorder, its signs, symptoms, and treatment methods.

Whether you personally suffer from bipolar disorder, or a family member or friend is afflicted, this book will be of some service to you.

You will soon discover the different symptoms and signs of bipolar disorder, as well as what can cause it, and trigger manic and depressive states.

You will learn about the different treatment options available, and be presented with a simple plan of action that you can take to improve the disorder.

This book will explain to you tips and techniques that will allow you to successfully understand, manage and treat your bipolar disorder condition in no time!

Bipolar disorder can be a difficult thing to live with, both for the sufferer and those around them, but it doesn't have to be this way. Follow the steps and advice provided in this guide and you will be well on your way to living a positive, healthy and happy life.

Thanks again for downloading this book, I hope you enjoy it!

Chapter 1 - Understanding Bipolar Disorder

Bipolar is taken from the compound word – "bi", meaning two and "polar", meaning sides, giving the apt description "two sides". In this medical condition, there are two opposing behaviors afflicting the individual. First is the manic phase where the person experiences an overwhelming feeling of happiness or euphoria. Second is the depressive phase where the person feels down, sad and suicidal. Hence, it is also called manic-depressive disorder.

Bipolar disorder is a disruptive, long-term condition, affecting men, women and even children, worldwide. An alarming estimate of 6 million adult Americans develop this condition each year. This number is also predicted to rise in the coming years. And, according to the study of the World Health Organization (WHO), bipolar disorder is the sixth leading cause of disability all over the world.

Science and medicine have yet to conclude what the real cause of Bipolar disorder is. There are predisposing factors though, leading to the development of this medical condition. These are the following:

1. Genetics. A person having blood relatives diagnosed with bipolar disorder is susceptible. The heritable component was validated when a study showed that two-thirds of the people with bipolar were

discovered to have at least one close relative suffering from it. The National Institute of Mental Health has placed the risk of a child developing bipolar disorder at 15-30% possibility when one parent is diagnosed. The risk is raised to 50-75% likelihood, however, if both parents have the disorder. The presence of certain genes in the family is said to be the cause of this inherent phenomenon.

2. Stress. Individuals whose tolerance for stress is lower than most people are more prone to develop this medical condition. Periods of high stress such as death of a loved one, a major loss or, a perceived failure in life, seem to trigger the conflicting behavior in an individual.

3. Chemical imbalance. Developing Bipolar Disorder has been linked to the disparity in numbers of the chemicals in the brain. These chemicals function as links to other domains of the brain such as emotions. Hence, when there is disruption in the "communication" of the neuro-circuit, an irregular response is obtained. The issue whether the chemical imbalance is congenital or acquired is yet to be settled.

4. Age. According to the study of the Depression and Bipolar Disorder Alliance, the average age of onset of bipolar disorder is 25 years old. However, it can also manifest in children as young as 9 years old and adults aged 40-50 years old. Why the young adults?

a. This is the age where one attempts to finish academic requirements, establish one's self as a professional, and have a family of his or her own. These events are all major milestones in life and are indeed, stressful. Plus, this is also the time when one usually experiences death of a loved one, especially that of grandparents or parents.

b. Young adults, at this time, are exposed to drugs, alcohol and other vices and they may be abusing these substances. Studies have linked these unhealthy habits to neurological severance.

One major key to a good prognosis of bipolar disorder is early detection. If you have any of these predisposing factors, it would be advisable that you undergo tests and consultations as soon as possible. The success rate of freedom from bipolar is increased in proportion to the early diagnosis, management and treatment of the disorder.

Chapter 2 - Detecting the Signs and Symptoms of Bipolar Disorder

One considerable difficulty of bipolar disorder is how to diagnosis it. Only about ¼ of all bipolar cases are being accurately diagnosed within three years. An extensive study revealed that people with bipolar usually take a decade of suffering before a correct diagnosis is achieved. Why the delay in the detection and diagnosis of this medical condition?

First, it is because bipolar is acquired and not congenital (inborn), in nature. Simply put, the person has no previous history or manifestation of any erratic or bizarre behavior that may warrant the suspicion of a mental disorder. They may have even been performing quite well before the development of the disorder. It is likely that early on they may have seemed "different" from others but there were no major indications of any deviation from the normal.

Second, the delay of detection could be because of denial - both of the person and of their immediate family. A mental disorder, of any kind and degree, has an attached stigma to it. That's why, even when the signs and symptoms are starting to manifest, not accepting the truth about the condition will inevitably delay diagnosis as well as treatment. And, like most kinds of mental illnesses, the tendency to worsen is increased in the absence of any management or treatment.

Third, the signs and symptoms are generic. Misdiagnosis is easy because of the similarities in symptoms. Depression is very common and is usually included in numerous mental disorders. What's more, symptoms of bipolar disorder like irritability, easy fatigability, inability to sleep, mood swings and loss of appetite, just to name a few, are common to a majority of the population. Hence, such manifestations are dismissed as just having a "bad day" or part of being "normal". It is only when the condition worsens that the person will go to the doctor for consultation.

Mania, Hypomania and Depression

The signs and symptoms will vary according to the type of bipolar disorder. Regardless of the type, there will always be episodes of depression and mania. Mania has varying degrees. Here is a comparison and contrast of mania and hypomania.

Mania is a symptom wherein the person feels a great excitement, unusual high energy, delusions and euphoria. If a person is in the manic phase, they will not be able to perform normal daily tasks. Other manifestations of mania are:

- There is a marked increase in energy. The person can go on and on without getting tired.
- Rapid speech and unusual talkativeness. They will speak incessantly in an uninterruptible manner. There is a flight of ideas and racing thoughts. Sometimes, in the middle of one thought, another idea will pop up and the person will just attach it to

the previous idea, leading to the confusion of the audience or the person they are talking to.
- Reckless behavior. An extravagant and out of line generosity to one's self and others will occur at this stage. The person may spend all their savings extravagantly. He or she may also engage in an inappropriate sexual relationship.
- Easily distracted. The person is unable to concentrate. They are too preoccupied with various things. There is no focus. They are unable to finish an assignment or a task before jumping to the next one.
- Exhibits impulsive, aggressive and erratic behavior. The person becomes so irritable that they pick a fight with anybody they come into contact with. Relationships are usually severed due to the erratic behavior. There is also poor judgment. For instance, quitting a job in a heartbeat.
- Lacks sleep and rest. The patient sleeps for 2-3 hours only. They can even manage to go without sleep the whole day and yet feel energized and active.
- Occasional illusions of grandeur are common. The person thinks they are superior from the rest of the population. There is no respect of opinions of others as he or she feels that his or her opinions are only those that matter.
- Having visual and auditory hallucinations. This is the perception of either seeing or hearing something that doesn't exist.

Hypomania, on the other hand, is defined as a lesser form of mania. All the manifestations in mania are present except for grandiosity, hallucinations, and psychotic symptoms. Another big difference is the ability of the person to function during a hypomanic phase. He or she is actually very productive, creative and excellent in his or her line of field, at this time.

Depression could occur before or after a period of mania or hypomania. Depressive symptoms can include:

- Feelings of hopelessness, sadness, helplessness, and emptiness.
- Inability to sleep and rest–The mind is in a state of unrest and chaos and is filled with unusually negative thoughts.
- Irritability – loss of patience. Mundane or petty things could lead to an explosion of temper and loss of control over situations.
- Loss of energy – physical and mental sluggishness. There is also a feeling of tiredness and easy fatigability in spite of being rested most of the time.
- Decreased or loss of appetite. The person will refuse to take in food or even think of eating at all.
- Thoughts of death and suicide. A depressed bipolar patient can be obsessed with thoughts of death. Usually, the person will directly inform other people of their intention of ending their life. When there is a possibility of committing harm to others or one's self, then rehabilitation is a must. Studies revealed that one out of five attempted suicides among bipolar patients is successful. The males have a

greater number of successful suicides while the females have an increased number of attempts. Studies also showed that the life expectancy of bipolar patient is reduced by 9 years compared to those without bipolar.

These symptoms could progress to severity if not treated. Again, early detection and diagnosis of the disorder is very vital as this could mean the difference between deterioration and recovery from bipolar.

Chapter 3 - Bipolar Disorder Treatment: Pharmacological Therapy

The cornerstone of treatment for bipolar disorder is pharmacological therapy. Success rates of early pharmacological treatment were previously estimated at 85%. However, adherence to this therapy is usually the issue as most patients complain of side effects, financial constraint and possible complications with long-term usage. Hence, full cooperation of the patient and the immediate family is needed to ensure that compliance to treatment is being observed.

Pharmacological treatment for bipolar disorder includes the following drugs:

- ➢ Mood stabilizers. Manages the ups and downs of one's moods. These drugs can be used both on manic and depressive phases. Lithium is the most popular mood stabilizer drug. It helps reduce the severity and frequency of mania while at the same time, relieves or prevents depression. Regular blood tests are required to monitor Lithium levels in the blood as Lithium can affect the kidney or thyroid function. Fluid intake of 8-12 glasses would also be recommended to prevent accumulation of Lithium in the bloodstream.

- Anticonvulsants. Originally intended for epileptic patients, these drugs were discovered to be effective in managing the mood swings of a bipolar patient. Used as mood stabilizers for the bipolar patient, these drugs can be given with or without Lithium to combat mania. Examples of anticonvulsant drugs are Tegretol and Lamictal.
- Antipsychotic drugs. This drug is usually combined with mood stabilizer drugs. They are used when the patient begins to manifest symptoms of hallucination and delusion.
- Other drugs. Benzodiazepines are fast acting sedatives found to relieve symptoms of insomnia and anxiety. Calcium channel blockers make good mood stabilizers, too.
- Antidepressants. A lot of medical practitioners question the use of antidepressants for bipolar. As hypomania and mania are the common manifestations of bipolar, giving the patients antidepressants may flip the situation of depression instantly and cause a manic phase instead. Observe extreme caution when using these.

Strict adherence to the pharmacological therapy is vital to the success of the treatment of this medical condition.

Here are general guidelines to observe during the therapy.

1. Medication is not the be-all, end all of treatment for bipolar disorder. Alongside pharmacological therapy, one should strive to do the other suggested

activities here and make changes in lifestyle to manage the symptoms.

2. Take the medication as prescribed. The physician's instructions should be strictly followed regarding when, how much, till when, and how to take the meds. There may be other special instructions about the drugs. Most importantly, continue the therapy even when the condition has markedly improved. This is the most common error of the patients. Do not discontinue the therapy without the doctor's knowledge or approval. Also, he or she should never self-medicate at any time.

3. Observe for side effects. As there are different responses to the drugs per person, finding the right combination of drugs may take time. The doctor usually monitors the effects of the drugs closely. The person can help the doctor by observing and reporting the symptoms, too. There are expected side effects and usually, the doctor would prescribe another drug to alleviate the side effect of the drug. However, one must watch closely for adverse reactions. These can be reactions that are not expected and should not be present at any time during the therapy. If there is any systemic reaction, they should immediately stop the therapy and report to the primary health care provider or go to the nearest hospital.

4. Be aware of drug interactions. Some medicines intended for the treatment of bipolar disorder may affect the effects of the person's other drugs, such as

maintenance meds for cardiovascular disease or other diseases, when taken together. The doctor must be informed of other existing medical conditions and their pharmacological management to ensure that there would be no conflict when all these medicines are administered to the patient at the same time.
5. Have a regular checkup and laboratory exams. Some drugs can cause toxicity to the kidneys and liver. The recommended schedule for blood work is every three months.

Pharmacological therapy can control the manic and depressive phases of bipolar disorder. A person can assume a normal life, have a career and a family, and make their dreams come true even if they are bipolar.

Chapter 4 - Non-Pharmacological Management of Bipolar Disorder

The latest trend in the treatment and management of bipolar is focused on non-pharmacological therapies such as psychotherapies combined with other complementary therapies. An astounding 86% improvement on the person's performance of tasks and activities of daily living as a result was recorded during a study. The implication of this result is the possible resumption of normalcy in a bipolar patient's life. Hence, medical practitioners are incorporating these non-pharmacological therapies into the management of bipolar also.

Psychotherapies for Bipolar Disorder

Here are some of the psychotherapies that could be administered together with the pharmacological therapy to increase the chance of good prognosis of the patient.

1. *Family therapy.* A strong support system is one of the keys to a successful treatment of bipolar disorder. Whether the patient lives with their family or not, the perception of support from them can strengthen the will to overcome the disorder. In the same manner, lack of support from the immediate family can lead to failure to achieve the targeted goal of treatment. Family therapy is focused on

2. stabilizing both the patient and their family through interaction, socialization and communication with one another. As the disorder can cause stress and distress on the whole family, having therapy as one unit can improve the way the family deals with the illness. It will be a great reminder to them that they are a team, designed to support and help one another. At the same time, finding a solution to whatever difficulty or challenge that they are facing because of this medical condition would not only remedy the problem but could bring them closer together. Indeed, this tool is very important in managing bipolar and easing the tension within the family. In this method, each member is encouraged to verbalize one's fears, concerns and issues. The bottom line of this therapy is this – a supportive home environment is crucial to the recovery of the patient from bipolar disorder and in assisting the other members of the family to cope with the challenges of the disorder.

3. *Group therapy.* A licensed or professional therapist will facilitate the meet up of different individuals suffering from this medical condition. The objective of the meeting is to improve the overall condition of the patient plus the other patients afflicted with the same illness, as they come together to discuss and share with one another their views and real life experiences with the illness. Seeing the insights of other people as well as verbalizing one's own

feelings can help the patient win their battle over the condition. For patients who are introverts and do not want to work with other people, there can be one on one interactions instead.

4. *Counseling*. Talk therapy is a vital tool in treating bipolar. The goal of this therapy is for the patient to manage the symptoms of bipolar through verbalization of one's feelings, leading to understanding and acceptance of one's self. As much as possible, only a skilled and experienced counselor should handle a bipolar patient. During the manic phase, there can be psychotic symptoms like auditory and visual hallucination. A skilled counselor will know how to respond to the perceived vision and sound of the patient. In delusion of grandeur, there is the superiority complex and manipulative behavior of the patient. Again, an experienced counselor would be able to curb the behavior without further damaging the mental state of the person. At the same time, aggressive behavior, suicidal tendencies and other manic-depressive symptoms would require expert handling to ensure the safety, not only of the patient, but of other people as well.

5. *Milieu Therapy*. The focus of this therapy is making the physical setting and arrangement of the environment therapeutic or helpful to the patients. For instance, during episodes of mania, the

patient's hyperactivity can hurt them due to falls, trips and bumps, as they engage in physical activities. This hyperactivity is a response to the excess energy that accompanies that phase. The environment then should be clutter-free and padded, if possible to keep the patient safe and free from harm. Meanwhile, during the depressive phase, thoughts of self-harm and death, usually fill the mind of the patient. Therefore, anything that can be used to hurt one's self and others should be removed from the surrounding.

6. *Cognitive-Behavior Therapy (CBT).* This therapy provides an opportunity for the patient to examine his or her thoughts and realize how those thoughts affect one's mood. Recognition of these thoughts and cessation from meditating them could lead to the recovery of the patient. While in this therapy, the skilled professional will teach the patient to change negative thinking patterns into positive ones. In effect, positive thinking will lead to more positive behavior. Cognitive behavior therapy has been proven effective in making the client more compliant to other therapies, improving client's perception of one's self and eliminating triggers for relapses.

7. *Play Therapy.* Used for children diagnosed with bipolar, this therapy aims to help the child express

their concerns, fears and other emotions through play.

The main goal of these psychotherapies is to assist the patient in understanding how to better manage the symptoms of bipolar by managing their thoughts and emotions.

Complementary Therapies

Aside from these psychotherapies, there are complementary therapies that are being utilized today. The term "complementary" is used to denote that these therapies are designed to be added to other therapies, for instance pharmacological therapy, to hasten the road to recovery. Here are some of the complementary therapies.

1. *Mindfulness meditation.* This therapy uses yoga, meditation and breathing exercises to encourage the patient to focus on the current situation. This is important during the manic phase of bipolar where hyperactivity is evident. It will assist the patient in concentrating on the task at hand. It is also used to help break negative thinking patterns of the patient and replace them with positive ones.

2. *Light and dark therapy* – In both manic and depressive phases, light and dark therapy would be able to provide sleep and rest to the patient. Reinforcing dark therapy for several hours could promote sleep and rest. One's mood could also

change because of light. How? Adjustment of the light to produce less brightness could provide calm to the chaotic state of the mind. On the contrary, during the depressed state, the light is adjusted to accommodate more light to uplift one's spirit.

3. *Acupuncture.* One predisposing factor for the development of bipolar disorder is stress. Acupuncture has shown to be effective in combatting stresses. It relaxes the person through pricking of needles in the skin in strategic places. Achievement of relaxation is expected to lessen episodes of mood swings.

Both psychotherapies and complementary therapies will speed up the recovery period of the patient. Choosing one or two of these therapies plus strict adherence to pharmacological therapy is crucial to the success of the treatment program for bipolar.

Chapter 5 - Self-Help Strategies For Bipolar Disorder

In the previous chapters, three approaches were discussed for the treatment and management of bipolar. These are pharmacological and non-pharmacological therapies, which include psychotherapies and complementary therapies. In this chapter, the most important key for the success of the disorder will be revealed and discussed.

The Secret Ingredient

Do you want to know what the secret ingredient to overcoming bipolar disorder is? The one that holds the key to recovery from bipolar is the person afflicted with it. There is nobody that can help them more than themselves. All the effective medicines and wonderful therapies are nothing without the cooperation of the patient. The patient themselves is the secret ingredient to the success of all endeavors against bipolar.

Here are some self-help strategies to combat bipolar disorder, gain back their quality of life and live the life that one deserves and wants.

1. Education. Knowledge about the enemy is the greatest weapon one can have. The person can take the upper hand against this disorder when they involve themselves totally. The goal is to learn everything about the disorder, from day one of the

diagnosis until the recovery period of the disease. One can avail information online, through the doctor, self-help groups and books, like this one.

2. Rediscover one's self. Bipolar is a really challenging disorder. However, when one is aware of their own strengths, weaknesses, and capabilities, they can face the enemy and win the battle. This can be achieved through rediscovering one's self. This is the process of finding out how one can push themselves against the impossible and emerge as the winner.

3. Empower one's self. Bipolar symptoms can be controlled even before they become full blown. Discover what causes the trigger in the first place and avoid it. Also, during the actual event that one is in the manic or depressive phase, be ready with practical tips on how to deal with the symptoms. Learn how to help yourself. However, do not value independence over safety. As soon as you know that you need help, then do seek help.

4. Compliance to the therapy. The person must try to comply to the therapies given, whether pharmacological or not.

5. Stress management. Stress can trigger bipolar. One can lessen episodes of bipolar by learning how to manage stress. There are many strategies that one can use.

a. Relaxation techniques – Learning proper breathing exercises can help control anxiety from rising. One can also do positive imagery. This is envisioning a positive image of one's self. There should be a healthy balance between work and play. Avoid all forms of negativity. Replace negative thoughts with positive ones. Yoga, meditation, mindfulness and other forms of rest could also provide a relaxed mind and body.
b. Music therapy – It can calm the mind and body. Music is therapeutic whether one is just listening, singing, humming, or playing an instrument.

6. Aim for a healthy lifestyle – When manic and depressive phases come, the person's appetite, sleep pattern, rest and activity are disrupted. To avoid complications, maintain a healthy body during the absence of the symptoms. When the symptoms appear, the body will not easily succumb to sicknesses. Also, unhealthy habits such as smoking, excessive alcohol consumption, poor diet and lack of sleep can trigger bipolar phases. If one's work is stressful, the person might want to be reassigned to a less stressful work environment if possible.

7. Believe in one's self. Bipolar symptoms and episodes could make one believe that a normal life is an impossible dream. Believe otherwise. Know that you have the ability to conquer this challenge.

One can live life to the fullest, with or without bipolar. Be free from the hold of this illness. You have what it takes to win this battle.

Chapter 6 - Living with Bipolar Disorder

To be diagnosed with bipolar may feel like it's the end of the line for you. You may feel hopeless, frustrated, angry and bitter especially when you can feel the symptoms. You feel out of control. There seems to be no way out.

Take courage. There is a way out. Bipolar disorder is truly a challenging condition. Nonetheless, it is not unconquerable. You can still be in charge of your life. Remember, you have what it takes to cope with the symptoms and enjoy a normal life with your family and friends.

Here are some of the things you can do when you are living with bipolar.

1. Accept it. It is not your fault. It is not your family's fault. It is nobody's fault. It will not do you any good to look for someone to blame for your condition. However, when you find the strength to accept it as part of being you, then there is hope that you can overcome it. If you just deny it, its existence will not cease. You will still feel the symptoms. Denying it will just delay the management. The sooner that you accept it and subject yourself to tests and management, the better your prognosis will be.

2. Deal with it. Never think that there is nothing that you can do. Face the disorder and deal with it. As suggested, get all the information you can about the disorder. Be objective and write down your observations. What are your feelings, what are the causes of your triggers, what should you do to control and manage the symptoms? Write down your plan of action.

3. Seek help. It is not a sign of weakness when you ask for help – both from a professional and from your family. Self-care is a very important aspect of bipolar management however it is understandable that there will be trying times. Do not carry everything on your own. Be especially sensitive to your personal safety and needs during depressive phases. If you are living alone, ask someone to stay with you or to stay with them temporarily until the worst of the depression is gone. Otherwise, you are endangering yourself, as this is the moments that you can have thoughts of hurting yourself. You could also opt to have yourself confined to rehabilitation if you have nowhere to stay and there is the possibility of committing suicide.

4. Comply with the treatment. To be knowledgeable of the importance of adhering both to the pharmacological and non-pharmacological therapies is beneficial for you. When you are not compliant to the treatment, you are subjecting yourself to possible complications. Your doctor is part of your team towards your road to recovery.

Give your full cooperation to your doctor.

5. Live a normal life. Do not think of yourself as hopeless and helpless. Do the usual tasks without forcing yourself too much. Remember, it is also not good for you to be stressed out. It will be better if you are able to establish a schedule or routine. Simplify life and remove the unnecessary dealings from your schedule.

6. Be ready for the symptoms. To be forewarned is to be forearmed. Do not be afraid but be ready with knowledge on how to manage them. Always have the number of your physician handy for any emergency.

7. Enjoy your life. The fact that you are breathing is something that should make you very glad already. Appreciate life. Look at your family and loved ones. Count your blessings. Be positive.

8. Enrich your life. Strive to do something better with your life. Continue growing and learning. Spend more time with your loved ones. Seek spiritual growth, too. Difficult times can be lighter when you have a faith to believe in.

Bipolar is not a hindrance to a great life. You can enjoy the life that you desire even if you are living with bipolar!

Conclusion

Thank you again for downloading this book!

I hope this book was able to help you learn more about bipolar disorder!

The next step is to put this information to use, and create a suitable treatment and management plan for your bipolar disorder.

Follow the steps in this book carefully, and you will be well on your way to conquering bipolar disorder!

Finally, if you enjoyed this book, please take the time to share your thoughts and post a review on Amazon. It'd be greatly appreciated!

Thank you and good luck!

www.ingramcontent.com/pod-product-compliance
Lightning Source LLC
LaVergne TN
LVHW021746060526
838200LV00052B/3502